Other Harbours

Anna Lewis was born in 1984. Her poems have been published in magazines including *Agenda*, *New Welsh Review*, *Poetry Wales* and *The Shop*, and were featured in the anthology *Ten of the Best* (Parthian, 2011). She has won several awards for her poetry, including the Christopher Tower prize and the Robin Reeves prize. In 2010 she won the Orange / *Harper's Bazaar* short story competition, and in 2011 performed at the Hay Festival and at literary festivals in Italy, Germany and Greece as part of the Scritture Giovani short story project.

Other Harbours

Anna Lewis

Parthian
The Old Surgery
Napier Street
Cardigan
SA43 1ED

www.parthianbooks.com

First published in 2012
© Anna Lewis 2012
All Rights Reserved

ISBN 978-1-908069-88-7

Editor: Kathryn Gray
Cover by www.theundercard.co.uk
Typeset by Elaine Sharples
Printed and bound by Dinefwr Press, Llandybie, Wales

Published with the financial support of the Welsh
Books Council.

British Library Cataloguing in Publication Data

A cataloguing record for this book is available from
the British Library.

Contents

Resistance

This is a town for old men:
they hunch down the pavements,
the shoulders of their jackets
rubbing thin against the walls.

The old men were boys here,
when this was a town for women
with headscarves tugged low,
with quick shoes, and quicker hunger.

This is a town for boys who
never left, who take the same steps
they took with their mothers,
the same boulevards and avenues

but slowly now; and so much,
and so little, has happened
since the soldiers bickering in pairs
on this corner, or that one.

Lights Off

'Attention! Dear comrades! The City Council informs you that due to the accident at Chernobyl atomic power station in the city of Pripyat there are adverse radioactive conditions... For these reasons, from 2pm today buses will be sent in... Comrades, temporarily leaving your residences, please close all windows, switch off electric and gas devices, and turn off water. Please observe calmness, organisation and order during this temporary evacuation.'

(Evacuation notice, Pripyat, Ukraine, 27th April 1986)

There was no flush of sea, no flames or ash,
no rats keeled over in the street.
An ordinary dawn and a southerly breeze;

we drank tea on the balcony,
watched the boys pedal figures-of-eight
in the courtyard below. Cars burred and
dogs lolled by the fountain, long-tongued –

it was that kind of morning: Sunday, spring.
Later that day, of course, we wedged holdalls
and rucksacks between our feet, and sat back
on black-and-brown tiger-print seats

as the coach eased away from the kerb,
with a faint stink of ashtray, sawdust
and trapped, rattled sun. At every corner
more coaches were boarding;

we lifted the kids to our laps to wave at
the windows, their lagoons of mirrored cloud.
And that was that. Taps tightened, lights off.

Keys turned and dropped in hip pockets
and one by one lost, or thrown out, or stowed
in dressers and chests in Kiev, in Malyn,

in Lutsk: reduced, as the locks they had fitted
rusted and froze, to a small shock of cold
at the back of a drawer.

Out of Town

A girl disappeared, not far from here,
from somewhere behind the Nepalese canteen,
the Cantonese minimart, the student bar
with flavoured vodka shots at three for two,
velveteen bean bags in the upstairs room.
Behind all these: an avenue of night-time mist
and close-pressed trees, lamp posts that hiss
and twitch, thick-curtained windows.
She went from there; but here, the narrow
pavements of the High Street overflow –
above the shops, girls call from sill to sill,
and from the doorways football scores
stream out, thin flags of bhangra, quick-
talking local radio. One less, one more:
no pale vacancy among the crowd,
no small cloud of silence.

*

From here the bus moves north, lumbers past
wide white drives of polished factories
and council office blocks, creaks at sparsely
flowered roundabouts, chevrons and arrows
snapping at each corner. A bridge,
a dell of nettles; then, a sagging barbed
wire fence, a ditch, fields of dandelion
and rusted troughs, earth trudged to mud

by herds no longer visible. The road pares,
trickles down to potholes, throbbing
storm-drains; street names limp from clots
of bramble. A village swerves around a bend,
trimmed with holly, jewelled throughout
with roadsigns: *Slow*, *Take Care*. The axels
bounce, the wheels shred yellow pools;
crows scoff above the fields.

*

Alight past the Huntsman, and take the first
right from the high road past the church,
cowering bungalows, last droop of apple
trees. The track grows broad and straight;
at the gatehouse wait, watch crows and magpies
pedal at the rolls of wire above the wall
and one by one admit defeat, retreat to
nearby leafless branches. It starts to rain.
When the man with clipboard shambles out,
try to pronounce the woman's name, and state
the business of your visit. Behind the walls
sequins of rain blend on the pond; stay,
again; and then a porch, a bare-floored lobby,
corridors, and finally a cubicle: two chairs,
one table, all nailed down. She sits across
from you and waits her turn to talk.

*

Every two hours the buses come, so you sit
in the stone shelter, read until the light has
truly gone, then stand and shuffle on the verge,
to stamp the cold into the ground. Over
the road: the closed-up pub, the church,
the curve of track toward the bungalows.
Beyond that you can no longer see, but know
the rooms you passed through must be empty
now, floors swept, litter plucked, chairs and
tables insignificant in shadow. Down the tiled
hall, the cells: in each a girl, a low bunk,
letters and pictures on the wall. Each life
is fixed in its allotted place, as in a train
that claws along a viaduct – each window
spilling out with light, the night's long
fall on either side.

The Dance

I can barely make it out. Death smiles, slim;
trips round the chapel walls in hand with
knights, bishops and market traders, chapped
and dim. Perhaps, beneath the newly painted

frescos, children kicked as a priest incanted,
rolled up their eyes and watched the dance
revolve, grew to know each face,
each separate Death skipping in white –

it's hard to concentrate. In a basin
of sunlight at the propped-back door
a beggar woman sits and calls, and calls,
as her children shriek on the outside steps.

We see her later, walking, hand outstretched
on Alexanderplatz between the S-Bahn entrance
and the television tower's enormous feet;
someone like her, again, on Kurfürstendamm,

with a brown-eyed baby in a pram – 'Speak English?'
the women say, and say; the baby has no language
yet, knows only crowd-sounds, cars and trams,
the frieze of faces far above his head.

Everything You Knew

Your Tokyo apartment was
flawless, or so you made it sound:
brisk walls, a kitchen that could scarcely

be entered with unshaded eyes;
and you, sifting your negatives
and prints on the floorboards,

monochrome cheekbones and
clavicles shaving your fingers –
those salt-white skins,

those tar lips.
In the Manchester rooms
where we met, you seemed

agitated by shadows, and sat
for hours by the window,
the whisper of a cigarette

between your fingers.
Sometimes you went out with
Brazilian friends, flared hair and

skirts, a chop of gold heels through
puddles – a Mitsubishi tablet or
two, which did nothing, you said,

and one time you brought home
a wordless boy, slight shoulders,
limp hands; you hunched

at the table in the blank
morning light, smoking,
quieter even than before.

You didn't take pictures here.
In the one that I took
you grin wildly, your mouth

and eyes huge: in negative
on the other side of the lens,
of everything you knew.

A Museum Education

In the snug of her neck

her bandages are torn, curled
where thieves urged fingers
at the snap of her skin.

As your breath thickens the glass,
you concentrate: the slow
carriages of your lungs, a pulse

in your fist. Here, above her
abdomen, was steatite; here faience;
carnelian against her breast. July

sprawls across the lobby floor,
smoulders in your palms and
the scoops of your knees;

gold pooling softly,
still liquid, warm.

The First Emperor

His logic slumps and flares,
a rank of bed sheets indelicately pegged to a line.
The immortal lands, he explains,
are but a little beyond the horizon –

as we keep watch in the dunes
he wades eastward towards evening,
water grey at his thighs,
the curling gulls pale above him.

Clouds part and close, reconfigure;
he is, for some moments, on course.

In Anatolia, Mary

All day under shade at the brink of the village,
she is still as the lizards on the orchard wall.

They barely breathe; a pulse flits
at the crux of their throats, bitumen

lifting under the sun. Their blood moves
more slowly than sun on the stones:

lichen seeds from the wall to their bellies
and weaves through their skins,

grapples their blue hearts, their lungs.
The day holds them in place.

At sunset she walks by the sea
with her back to the east,

as birds cloud the cove, and dusk closes
a door on the narrowing black of her dress.

The Doors

The doors stumble apart
and we enter a nave scarred
with moonlight, where long windows
spill tongues down black walls.

Candles pressed in our palms
we progress to the saints on the rood,
to their splintered hands, puckered haloes:
tin bowls worn through.

We plant our flames and present
our bowed heads. The babies stutter
at our chests. Behind us, those
with their hands held loose,

those who carry only a cold and
bolted room, cross their hearts with
prayers of their own making;
then rise and follow us back

down the aisle, through the mass
of wet, grey grass at the step,
towards the low pate of first sun.

Last Light

(i) Arawn's Wife

The nights have changed shape.
The first is long and narrow.
Arawn's wife lies on her side,
stares at the back of her husband's head,
measures the spool of his breath.
An hour passes before she sleeps.

Weeks. The nights tighten:
she kicks at her husband's legs,
stammers his back with her hands,
asks his shoulders again and again
why he has changed.
He ignores her; she cries; her days
are stiff with tiredness. She is taut
with her maids, suspects each in turn.

Months, and the nights draw back.
Moonlight is usual now,
soothes her, a distant music.
She trails the curve of his neck
with quiet fingers.
She cries a little, still,
her body weighed down
with useless organs, bulky cushions of flesh.

The third season slows to the fourth
and the nights are shallower,
young waves in a retreating tide.
He tells her his dreams in the
mornings; she tells him hers.

(ii) Teyrnon's Wife

If you are lying, I can't tell.
You sleep deeply, eat heftily;
each pocket of your body still
clasps its old scent.
                              In privacy
your fingers drawl my back,
their pace and pressure unchanged –
and your lips buffing my shoulder,
the rough of your knee parting mine:
all as it should be.

But through my narrow window
I watch the child mimic you in the field,
the sun's low sweep. His shadow
shakes into yours, keeps to its line.
That night, when you knocked at
my room – *I have found a boy,*
if you will keep him –

something came loose in me.
Now, you say, you have an idea
of his mother: the Lady who waits
by the horseblock at her husband's gate,
and carries strangers to court, in penance
for losing their child.

You don't invite me there with you.
I would have ridden her, the mare,
and spurred her for good measure;

only, I never want to know
the saddle of her hips under mine,
the charge of her breasts against my hands.

(iii) Manawydan

I have worn her down:
I mused for hours on outsoles and uppers,
pondered over this leather or that –

I made her test the tread of my shoes,
chased and counted her footsteps, and now
I don't know where she walks; my stitches won't hold.

It hurts to think of the flex of her feet as she moves:
the arches as they hitch and flatten,
the flicker of those birch-bones under the skin.

I have heard that in some fantastic, faraway land,
they break and fold the feet of small girls
and bind them in silk,
making their women exquisite, and lame;

and I dream of Rhiannon,
bandaged and bloodied, twisting
on a strange forest floor, as cherry blossom falls
and gathers in drifts, a red snow.

(iv) Llwyd's Wife

For weeks, I have worried
that you will be born a timid,
snuffling thing, fraught with dreams

of wheat fields high as forests,
of giants who loom towards you,
a gape of huge hands.

You drift at the end of my blood:
every picture, each word,
taps a code down this cord

to you poised,
wide-eyed in the dark as a sentry
and ready; receiving, receiving.

(v) Aranrhod

My brothers each come with the other;
you may call either one by each name.
Wolf: boar. One held down the girl

while the other held shut the door.
Their punishment: spines horizontal,
a gallop of rock and wet moss

underneath hoof and paw, eight strong
legs and two hearts bound in fur;
three years in rain, three years

on the mud of the woodland floor.
Nights when one hid from the other,
listened and hunched still:

owl-call, rabbit-scream, silence,
a rush of dead leaves.
Even after all this

one arrived at my gate, clean-shaven,
a twisting child in his arms.
Uncle: father. That smile.

(vi) Goewin

He has made his peace with my husband.
They embrace in our hallway,
and I sit with them both at table.

He is here for a favour: a bride for his son,
and the men select oak flower, meadowsweet, broom.
They take turns to pluck, thread and twist
until their hands slide with juices,

until, at last light,
they coax a girl from carpels and stamens,
from sepals and slender petals.

She stands naked between them,
skin sticky with sap,
breasts still swelling from her chest.
Their tips firm and ripen, dark as fumitory.

North

Giso of Lorraine: Bishop of Wells, Somerset, 1061–88

They call it the country of summer
but summers here are short,
and fringed with water.
                                There are stories
of women who crouch in the caves,
made deaf by rivers blasting a pass
through the rock –
                                half-blind in the miles
of darkness, and dumb, they shunt closer
to stone with each year.

                                They need him, here.
Lorraine was a childhood, green and gold,
threaded with thick rivers, deep days
full of sun.
                                In the nave he shields
his candle and walks, the choir with
flames and bells at his heels. He kneels
at the altar,
                                lifts his voice while outside
the wind bores at the limestone walls:
a long torso of water far underground,
sightless, burrowing up to the light.

Seed

At the plague's height, when life
continued as normal in many respects,
but people died more frequently,

and the town stank constantly
of something like raw meat, or rotten vegetables,
there was neither space nor time for proper burials,

so earth was lifted from the Green in cartloads
and the healthy slung the dead into the pit:
farmhands shovelling wet mounds of leaves.

After the Green was filled and trampled down,
and grass was sown and paths were worn,
the choir returned; as they rehearsed,

their voices tasselled at the shoulders
of the women in the market, and the traders,
and the rings of children spinning on the Green,

who laughed and fell, and scrambled up, still laughed
as they brushed the grass and soil from their knees.

Powder

5th November, 1605

Thirty years earlier, it might have soothed –
but, blurred to a dirge, his mother's lullaby
struck hammer-weight against the inside of his skull.

He tugged each footstep from the shadows,
clammy as oil on the floor.
Stiff at the centre of his lantern's globe,
he watched each inch of wall drone into light
and back to shade; the passage narrowed,
the ceiling tamped at his hair.

The lullaby repeated, slower than before.
In the lantern's ever-closer flame,
he thought he saw –

                    and didn't see, and thought again –
the swing of dancers in the corridor,
blooming, retreating in the swivel of each eye.
As though asleep: his feet deep, deeper in the ground,
the cramped passageway,

and then the tinder and the ready fuse,
the lamplight wide again;

                    the sudden noise,
half in the head and half without,
the steady hand that shakes the shoulder.

Blue

The fields had stood bald for months:
the earth tight with ice, the tubers
and kernels stashed below locked

fast inside their rinds. Then the hair
had started to fail on the children,
their nails to turn blue as the frost

that spotted the leaves, and the cow
would no longer yield but had stalled
in the dust, refused to rise.

So the parents had nailed shut
the door and carried the children,
light as shaken-out sacks, to the town.

From the almshouse walls they watched
clouds stiffen over the sea, thought of
the boarded door, the sealed ground.

They had left too late for their daughter:
wrapped in white, she was blessed in
the chapel as her brother looked up,

up into the dome, tipped the back
of his head to his shoulders, filled
his eyes with the ceiling's empty bowl.

Transmission

Jean-François Champollion (1790–1832): the principle translator of the Rosetta Stone.

The road's cold incline into Grenoble
lifts him, bears him foot by sullen foot
towards an air that shreds to tissue in his lungs.

At the doorstep of the lodging house
he kicks one shoe against the other,
claps loose the snow within the treads.

An hour, two, in the white-walled parlour
while the adults talk, then he is shown
to his high room, his bed, a blanket

of stubbled Alpine wool.
He won't blow out his candle,
but as it nips and hisses by his head,

watches the flex and steal of fissures
on the ceiling – just as, south-east across
the sea, the Nile webs the delta

where the stone was lifted, sand
knocked from its ruts and grooves.
He shivers: wills the snow to melt.

China

It seemed innocent, somehow:
a blossom of foam in the gutters,
soap's frail scent

in a canopy over each street,
so much kinder than most
smells of war. Less delicate:

the fresh dew of glass each
morning, the broken patterns
of sleep, hours watching

flowers grow sharp on the wall,
waiting for footsteps to chip
night's blue gloom.

It was a war of soapsuds
and china in the streets;
on bare docks, men squared

under cloudless skies.
Their shadows spilled over
the quay, ran into each other

as ships gripped the tide,
drove anchors down through
the fracturing waters of the bay.

Lesson

'Alas, poor Yorick,' said Peter as he knelt, and attempted
to fit his hand round the skull's grey bulb –
but at its back, the bone had fused to the rock,

so Peter rested his hand as a doctor feels for fever,
his little finger draping the nooks of its eyes.
Miss Harrow pulled us back; drew her cane, tick-tick,

over the ribs and the pelvis, tapped each leg bone
and arm bone in turn. We jigged and pushed
for position on the mush of sand.

The diagnosis was made by Miss Steele at the schoolhouse:
in Krakatoa's wreck, the poor soul had stuck
to the hardening lava and floated, merged to pumice stone,

washed up on our Zanzibar the year after.
From Sumatra, most likely, where in a moment
the air had ignited, and an ash-black wind

had swung through windows and doors. We nodded,
watched our old Mr. Bones spin and beam on his strings.
'Say a prayer for them, boys,' said Miss Harrow.

Peter read: 'I will never forget you; I have held you
in the palm of my hand. Isaiah 49: 15-16.'
In the East Indies, we had heard, they thought that Allah

was angry, that mouth after mouth blamed the Dutch.
'No,' said Miss Steele, 'God did not desert them.
From Hell He has delivered them here, cool, to us.'

The Paternoster

i

Warsaw – Dubno
September 1939

Ankles clamped to your suitcase,
thighs numb under the sag of the bag on your lap,
you keep pace with the sway of your face in the window,
your lips and nose franked on the drab southern fields.

The window divides you:
you are the boy on his bench in the carriage,
sleep flaking and knotting, muslin-thin, in his head;
you are his twin who bumps over the cornrows and
        furrows,
the streams and plank bridges.

On the last limb of track into Dubno,
sun outscores the carriage's lamp.
Among engine sheds and tenement backs
the twin disintegrates, scrapes into brick and
        blackened boards;

between carriage and platform, still wispy with sleep,
you descend from your old Warsaw door to the street.

ii

Dubno – Fălticeni
September 1939

The lawns are all torn up,
the walls reduced to rockeries,
trees split at the trunk.
Rats have the run of high street, town square, market hall.

The news comes through in tributaries: garbled, polluted.
You can't be sure.
The glass animals that lined your bedroom shelf –
cow, pig, marvellous elephant – either lie in sandy heaps
or stand, but dim with ash and dust.

Their loss hurts stupidly.
In Fălticeni, safely south of the frontier,
you play mud-footed in the fields,
outwit a cow with scythe-sized horns –
but night after makeshift night, you dream of your
        menagerie,
its transparent parade along your wall.

Your car, weighted with soldiers – boot, running board
and bonnet – was among the last across the border.
Those who left Dubno five, ten minutes too late

wait, still wait, line the south-bound roads,
bellies vacant, faces set. Their veins and bones
make themselves known against the skin.

iii

Craiova – Paris
December 1939

Below the drawn bow of the Carpathians, the Jiu
        chimes south,
more rowdy with every hour toward winter.
The days shut into each other;
an almost-blue moon skims the turrets and steeples
as snow blanches your footprints through Romanescu
        Park.

One afternoon, you return from school
blowing over your fingers, and your mother
shakes a paper at you in the hallway:
Visa! Like viva – vita – life.

Steaming west, your palms are grooved red
from the handles of crammed-up cases,
your mother curses late trains and missed connections,
grinds her teeth to the catch of wheels

and Paris topples in through the windows, draped
and shuttered, pigeons wetly clumping in gutters.
Chestnut vendors hail you in the street;
your suitcase slams your legs.

That afternoon, from the window of your room
in the Hôtel Perreyve, you watch rain drill the
        pavements,

a flurry of bowed, covered heads;
press the looming bruise on your shin
and feel the ache like a bell call: awake! awake!

iv

Paris – St. Jean de Luz
June 1940

Rain hangs above the beach in slats.
The Basque lands, the Bay of Biscay: so luminous,
your mother assured you in Paris,
as you folded your shirts down into their creases
and strapped shut the case –

but above your quiet crowd the clouds are sour;
a loose tarpaulin sea flaps beyond the harbour wall,
and chairs and tables tilt along the tideline,
legs snapped with weed. At the highest table
two officers sit: one French, one British,
hands stout about near-empty bottles,
a damp scurf in their ashtray.

The ships will take no more; behind their hides,
soldiers slide rosaries between their fingers.
The last anchor lifts.
Your sole hope, now, is the tentative road south:
the Pyrenees, the charmed waters of Lourdes,
Toulouse, the rumour of the free zone.

As you swarm the coast road's dozen empty trucks,
load yourselves up to the pallets, the officers
smoke slowly on their awkward chairs,
and lean and lean into the sand.

v

Grenoble – Gibraltar
September 1943

On your way to the station, you weren't supposed
to turn or wave but did, once, cleanly,
as though away to lectures or on errands,
your mother's hand at half-mast in the window.

All the way across the square's remainder,
its sudden miles, you felt the soldiers watch you.
Their smoke webbed your coat as you
walked the length of the river

where, that summer gone, you'd rowed,
where odd boats still nagged at their tethers.
Above your head the gulls still swung
and you thought on to Andorra, Barcelona,

to Gibraltar, where you'd step from the jetty
and deck would shift under your feet: that gap
where continents rise and decline on each side
and you, for a while, might buoy between.

vi

It was not that you decided,
once ringed by this island's cliffs and currents,
that you had seen the last of lorry holds,
of sleeper trains and midnight convoys –
you simply didn't leave, and kept not leaving.

After the war was done with, and Europe
closed like a greatcoat,
your parents returned to Paris, took rooms off the rue
    d'Assas,
shopped once more in the Marché St. Germain.

They thought you might join them, but you didn't go,
and keep not going.
Between morning seminar and staffroom,
you pass the doorless cars of the paternoster
where they lift and fall beside the lobby,

and pause daily to wonder at its riders:
arms snug with books,
feet leaping the threshold without hesitation.

The Catch

Lir's children are drawn up
as though by threads from the plinth
and into their story, arms tensed
for the itch and sear of new feathers,
for the catch of first flight. Think
        of the quick, blunt thrust
of quill through skin, seedlings
cleaving wet earth; lips clench,
rigid; fingers won't part. They churn
by the pool in Parnell Square,
noonday sun crisp on the water;
                it is September.
East of the city, ferries crease
the bay; shudder from harbour,
the earth's pull let slack.

Lungs

The sky pressed onto the field, a bellows,
squeezed the same stale air back and forth

until earth cracked like old leather, and the roots
and tendrils that knotted together the soil
split and shrivelled, started to come undone.

Soldiers no longer ran low through
the vines – the trip lines were wound
in, the mines uprooted –

but rumours came down from the village
of children with breath stuck in their chests,
unable to move from their beds;

or walking but pulling one dead
leg behind them, small bodies mauled
as though by guns or gas or wire.

On the *domaine* they kept off the road,
and lay through limp nights with shutters
latched, the field a bristle of crickets

and frittering leaves; fenced from sleep
by wind in the trees at the roadside,
the downhill march of the stream.

Ohka

Okinawa, 1945

Yokosuka Ohka: named for a sweet fist of petals,
for cherry blossom unravelled through April skies.

The flower sprayed against its fuselage
tenses: an open hand. The pilot arches

over his knees; his back stiffens, breath refuses
as blossom twists from the tree – Ohka,

by the hundred, hooks to the breeze
and the ocean comes out in bloom, flinches

through crimson to pink: petals turned
by the wind over Aoyama Park in spring.

The Wash-house

They knotted roots and wild petals together,
waved their hands in some fashion or other,
and this droop of a girl sat up from the green.

A bride for the groom. She doesn't say much:
words teeter out like young shoots.
'Don't remember,' she says,
so I show her where she used to be broom,
where she hitched herself from the dry soil under the cliff,
allowed bees to fuss at each cup.

I show her where she was meadowsweet,
where she thickened the low field by the stream:
where, always thirsty, she insisted her roots
in tough currents downwards,
wrangled the earth.

I show her where she was oak flower,
where she pouted in gangs between the spring twigs,
urged a green thud of water up through the trunk,
into those thousand pink mouths.

'Next?' she says, wheeling hair round her finger,
but we are due back at the hall.
We stand for a few moments longer,
watch blossom spin over the stream.

ii

I help her tighten herself every morning,
tense the hinge of each elbow, each knee.
She's all tendril, no sinew, apparently,
inclined to wilt,
unable to hold up her eyelids past dusk.

Bees clot at her armpits, and the back of her neck.
I swat them away, shake pollen grains
from her sheets. She complains
that all her food tastes of honey.

I feed her spoonfuls of salt,
give her garlic cloves whole.
I set candles in a throng round her pillow;
still, she tastes only sugar,
sleeps from sunset until dawn.
Each morning, I scrape cold wax from the floor.

We stretch, bend, stretch; she gets limper
as August shrinks to September,
and the first autumn fire blurts in the hall.

iii

The leaves have burnt out
and we all settle down to our snow-pace,
darn and patch up the woollens,
salt and cure small game.
I don't see so much of the girl –
her husband away, she keeps her door bolted,
won't meet my eye when we pass in the halls.

But we've had her pegged, in the wash-rooms and
        kitchens,
since the first crocus burst up through the frost,
since snapdragons circled the banks of the frozen pond,
and plums tumbled over white ground.

It gets no warmer,
sunlight shallow and brief on the field.
Her door bangs at midnight, and again before dawn;
she sleeps later, talks faster, flagrant
as the clematis limbering over her window.

iv

She said nothing when she brought me her laundry,
the dress bloodied, stuck with wet feathers.
In the heat and fat steam of the wash-house
I powder the stains with salt grains and soap flakes,
as suds billow pink at my knuckles.

I imagine them both hand in hand by the stream:
a faint stroke of cloud, dew on the grass.
She is jubilant, luminous as a pasture after strong rain.

I said nothing when she brought me her laundry,
her rose-hip lips twitching;
I scrub through the steam,

see him lean down for a kiss, see her step aside
as the blade shivers quick from the bushes,
startles a red brace of wings from his chest.

V

But blood of his calibre can't be dismantled –
a limb, once pulled from these people, grows back.
He'll be gathered from the high branches
by well-practised hands,

and she will be blamed, with each crooked step
as he lurches towards his old shape:
as he shakes out his fingers,
rights his spine bone by bone,
shrugs dead wings from his shoulders.

He'll brush off the feathers,
grapple each hand to a fist.
The tilt of his spine unlocked and inclining,
he'll stamp a path home through the clover,

                         the low blooms.

vi

Odd evenings, I offer to fetch firewood from the copse.
On my way, I pinch scraps from the kitchen –
just cuts of fat, or green meat – slice them small,
leave them under the nearest oak to the stream.

Sometimes she gobbles them down;
other times circles and pecks, totters off.

She is much the same as when first at the court:
unsure on her pins, pluck-plant-plucking
her way through the field; and quiet,
huge-eyed, with pupils that flit in the breeze.

Hard to say how she's changed:
not so gaudy, easy to lose in the autumn leaves,
as once she could dissolve into blossom,
and high meadow grass.

I never stay long; curtsey and turn back to the hall,
a bundle of dry twigs under each arm.

Mr. Flat-head

As you drop from the lorry's underside
and its back wheel jolts over your head,
flattening your skull,

you think perhaps of home, or God,
or nothing much:
the road, the noise, the long second of shock.

It doesn't matter now;
not to the forensic team,
who collect the hundred fragments
of your head, sponge them clean
of blood and hair,

who piece you back together,
build you up in wax and plaster,
who name you, and chat to your breezy,
loose-toothed grin.

Your family recognise the face;
the work is done.
If you had finished your journey,
you'd be stooping now

in a Devon field, gathering daffodils,
pausing every other bundle
to hitch your hood against the rain.

Homecoming

When it was over, papers signed
and witnessed, berths arranged,
some of the men sailed back

to villages where hens still laid
and bells still swung and nuns,
in steady order, still stepped
down and down the aisle

but where, all the same, the pitch
of life had changed: houses empty,
fields overgrown, blots of black ink
pooled in the congregation.

Some men did not go back to that,
nor to the factories, or harbour towns
where cats and gulls fought over scraps
on oily seafronts; some men descended

from the barns where they'd been held
and learnt the language, charmed the girls,
sent invitations to their parents.
Above the town, they raised a stone plinth

with a wolf on top, two infants suckling;
lifted a glass of wine to Rome
and to life climbing on, and walked their
children up the verge to show them;

but hot with nettle stings, palms sweaty,
the children whined for lemonade,
said, 'It looks more like a bear,'
and wanted to go home.

Tibet

You grind upwards,
as a climber grinds upwards with ice pick and spurs.
Near vertical, you do not look down,
the snow cramping and griping around you,
a white needle of wind in each ear.

There is not much space for people like you,
between the tramlines and the newsstands,
the straight-faced joggers
in the Parc de Bruxelles:

all the world's corners fit flush together,
and you think, *I am alone in my corner*,
as you watch the boxers dance and embrace
in newly blue and red technicolour –

but your thoughts are in white and you walk
by the fountain, where the lovers
glide past in pairs;

                          and then you are home,
two hands on one rail,
pulling yourself up the stairs
as a climber pulls on a rope,

and your heartbeat is white,
your lungs full of white, and the door
to your bedroom stands open,

a woman reaches out from the linen,
but she is cold to your touch
and from the neck up she is smooth,
featureless, a field under snow.

Penelope

The ancient Britons never did it for me –
their mudded veg and dowdy wattle-and-daub,
accents that furl up into our own –

but the Greeks ran me through, a virus:
Daphne skirted the trip-wires of my bronchioli,
the Minotaur hoofed at each turn of my gut
and Odysseus wrested his oars down my arteries,
winier, blacker, than any Greek sea.

Their scandals distracted me;
I feared turning bad, as a pear does,
from the core to the skin

and I wished for it,
biting my neatly filed nails at the front of the class,
swinging, swinging my legs from the stool,

as I waited to be re-made by love,
to understand what made the Minotaur steam in his
        cave,
why Apollo pounded for miles after Daphne,
what made Odysseus flounder

for so long with Circe,
as Penelope paced at some other harbour
baring herself, day after day,
to the scrape of each empty incoming tide.

Breath

Our mother calls it ozone: the green sour breath
that wells up from the bay, rises from salt,
heaped seaweed, trapped drabs of water.

We stalk from rock to rock –
the weed's wet blisters pop beneath our feet,
and we hang our shadows from our shoulders,

crouch, wait. Wait, then dip –
our buckets squirm with crabs,
broad-footed beetles, ghostly shrimp.

Our shadows shrink. We tip the swimming things
back to their niches, lift our weed-stuffed buckets
to our faces, and breathe in.

After dark, craneflies tatter the walls of our strange
bedroom. Lace scuds white at the window
as tight ferns and night-flowers, colourless,

unwind their necks around the edges of the garden.
You sleep, the craneflies sleep;
by the chest of drawers, our buckets squeak and sigh.

The Cows

One night, my sister and I shared the same dream:
a black herd of cows shouldered in from the porch,
udders thick and ropey as bell-pulls,
bellies low, ankles trim;

they hefted the long hulls of their bodies
through the hall, the kitchen, our twin bedroom.
After that, for a while, we feared the herd
in the neighbouring field. We thought

we could lay a grid at our door, and imagined
the cows in a steaming crowd at its lip: how
they'd grumble with milk and rich, red flesh,
thresh the ground with their narrow hooves

and yet be held back, as though by a magnet's
invisible push: how they'd dread the next step,
their own sudden weight.

Excavation

It's over now: the land patched up,
seams in the turf prepare to heal,
as six o'clock sunlight settles

like a gauze. And the cows are back,
nudging the trampled grass, where
yesterday arrows and strings pinned

open the earth, its private geometry
raw beneath the sky. The grass will
grow paler here, next spring; already

shadows begin to charge their steady
angles through the field, test its
new and tender contours.

Notes

The First Emperor
Qin Shihuangdi, the first emperor of China, was obsessed with finding an elixir for eternal life. He died in 210 BC, allegedly from mercury consumed in his quest for immortality.

Last Light
This sequence gives voice to some often-overlooked characters from the medieval Welsh *Mabinogion*:

Arawn's Wife
Arawn, a king of the otherworld, trades place and form for one year with another man, Pwyll. Arawn does not tell his wife.

Teyrnon's Wife
Teyrnon finds and raises an abandoned child, probably the missing son of Pwyll and his wife Rhiannon, at whose court Teyrnon once served.

Manawydan
When the magician Llwyd casts a spell over Dyfed, emptying it of all life, Manawydan must travel to England and take work as a shoemaker. His wife Rhiannon, Pwyll's widow, later vanishes.

Llwyd's Wife
Manawydan turns Llwyd's pregnant wife into a mouse. She is captured, and narrowly survives.

Aranrhod
Aranrhod refuses to acknowledge her illegitimate son, who was raised by her brother Gwydion. Gwydion and his brother were, previously, turned into animals as punishment for rape.

Goewin
Goewin's husband forgives his friend Gwydion for Goewin's rape.

Transmission
At the age of around ten, Jean-François Champollion was sent to school in Grenoble, where he dedicated himself to the study of ancient eastern languages. The Rosetta Stone had been discovered some twenty years earlier. Champollion later made the linguistic breakthrough that enabled Egyptian hieroglyphics to be decoded.

China
In the 1911 dockworkers' strike, Chinese strike-breakers were brought into Cardiff Bay. This resulted in attacks on the local Chinese community, particularly on laundries and restaurants.

The Catch

In Irish folklore, the Children of Lir were turned into swans by their stepmother. A statue depicts them in Dublin's Parnell Square.

The Wash-house

This sequence is drawn from the story of Blodeuedd, found in the *Mabinogion*. Blodeuedd, thought to represent the natural world in human form, is created by magic from wild flowers to be the bride for a nobleman, but begins an affair with another man who encourages her to kill her husband. Their attempt at murder fails when her husband transforms into an eagle, and flies out of sight. Blodeuedd's husband is later reinstated by his uncle, Gwydion, who pursues Blodeuedd, and turns her into an owl as punishment for her disloyalty.

The sequence is told from the imagined perspective of Blodeuedd's maid.

Acknowledgements

Thanks are due to the editors of the following publications, in which some of these poems first appeared: *Agenda*, *Cheval*, *Modern Poetry in Translation*, *New Welsh Review*, *Poetry Wales*, *The Shop*, *Tower Poetry Review* and *Ten of the Best* (Parthian, 2011).

The sequence 'The Paternoster' was inspired by the memoirs of my grandfather, Janusz Grodecki.

Large parts of this collection were written with the assistance of a bursary from Literature Wales, for which I am very grateful. I have benefited also from the support of Tower Poetry, Tŷ Newydd and the Welsh Writers Trust, and would like to thank everyone I have met at the Dylan Thomas Centre, Swansea, for their encouragement and friendship.

Many thanks to my editor, Kathryn Gray, for all her astute and thoughtful advice.

Finally, for their careful reading and discussion of many of these poems, I would like to thank my parents Stephen and Barbara, my sister Philippa and my partner Rhys.